UN
READING ASSOC

MINI BOOK SERIES   No 6

Supporting Struggling Readers

Diana Bentley   Dee Reid

MINI BOOK SERIES

Series Editor   Alison B. Littlefair

No. 1   Genres in the Classroom, Alison B. Littlefair

No. 2   Running Family Reading Groups, Sue Beverton,
         Morag Hunter-Carsch, Cecilia Obrist, Anne Stuart

No 3   Miscue Analysis in the Classroom, Robin Campbell

No 4   Teaching Handwriting, Peter Smith

No 5   Teaching Spelling, Brigid Smith

Issue No. 6:   Supporting Struggling Readers

Issue Authors: Diana Bentley and Dee Reid

ISBN 1 897638 09 4   ISSN 1350-7664

Published by: United Kingdom Reading Association
             c/o Warrington Road County Primary School
             Naylor Road, Widnes, Cheshire WA8 0BP, England

April 1995

British Library Cataloguing in Publication Data. A catalogue record for this book
is available from the British Library.

Contents

SUPPORTING STRUGGLING READERS

A disappointingly high number of children enter Y3 with only limited reading skills. Although early years teachers have been concerned about these children during their first two years in school this concern increases dramatically after assessment at end of Key Stage 1.

The reasons for their lack of progress are likely to be as varied as the children themselves. The system of Statementing children with learning difficulties through the Code of Practice inevitably means that many children with reading problems are not entitled to receive expert help from the outside agencies. These children are the sole responsibility of the classroom teacher.

Finding effective means of remediation is an on-going concern in both primary and secondary schools. As the children get older the gaps tend to widen between what they are able to achieve with their limited reading ability and what they are expected to achieve in the classroom. This lack of reading ability holds back progress across the curriculum as all subjects eventually demand sophisticated reading skills and children who have difficulty understanding the written word and who have weak decoding skills find it almost impossible to participate in a full curriculum.

What do struggling readers think reading is?

"Reading is the process of turning written language into meaning"
Meek (1991)

Competent readers know what reading is but struggling readers frequently stress the decoding of individual words at the expense of comprehending the meaning of a text.

When struggling readers are asked what they think reading is and why they think reading is important they frequently reveal that they gain little pleasure from reading and suggest that reading has very little importance in their lives. The following comments were collected from a group of children in a primary school and their responses are typical of children who find it difficult to read with any fluency:

"Learning about words" (Julian aged 10)

"Learning words" (Tod aged 8)

"Learning" (Michael aged 11)

"I'm a bit stuck on that one" (Alex aged 8)

"No talking, most of us sits and read a book but the boys doesn't" (Claire aged 9)

"Umm...... hard" (Luke aged 8)

Children who find reading difficult often have a very inadequate view of the reading process. They may be aware that reading involves word recognition; they may have a hazy notion of the connection between the sound of thé letter and its position within the word, but they do not connect these skills into the wider notion of making meaning from the printed word.

If children are to make genuine progress they have to realise that what they are reading on the page represents a message to which they must respond. Teachers are aware that this inadequate view of reading hinders progress but nevertheless the temptation to concentrate solely upon improving the skills of reading means that this vital ingredient is often neglected.

The work of Stanovitch (1980) pointed out that fluent readers use very little processing capacity for word recognition and therefore are able to pay much more attention to interpreting the words on the page. By contrast poor readers need to use all their processing capacity for decoding. They spend time endeavouring to recognise the letters and then try to associate these with the relevant sounds. As a result these children have very little processing capacity left with which to comprehend the text.

Rapid word recognition and phonic knowledge are vital ingredients for reading success but if the context of the words is not also absorbed then the reader is doing no more than "barking at print."

The dilemma facing the teacher is finding the balance between teaching the necessary skills and ensuring that the child with reading difficulties is immersed in reading experiences which stress the cohesion of text and the continuity of story.

In 1990 Jane Medwell undertook a small scale piece of research into children's perceptions of the reading process. She found that poor readers expressed their concept of reading only in terms of decoding and word recognition. They made the greatest use of grapho-phonic information in their reading and very little use of semantic cues. She found that good readers of the same age described reading as enjoyable, they understood **why** they read and what the outcomes of the reading should be. The good readers made less use of the grapho-phonic cues and used context to predict unfamiliar words.

It is therefore very informative to discover children's perceptions of what reading is and their attitude towards it. A poor attitude may be contributory to their lack of success, it is part of their reading problem and a favourable attitude should be part of the solution. It is essential that every opportunity is taken to ensure that children with reading difficulties partake in "whole" reading activities and that any remedial programme takes account of this.

"Readers are made when they discover the activity is "worth it". Poor, inadequate readers lack literary competence because they have too little idea of what is "in" reading for them." Meek (1991)

The importance of observation

Before teachers can really expect to help a child effectively they need to make careful and detailed observations about the attitude and skills of the child in question. There may be extensive records from a school or teacher but sometimes these seem to bear little resemblance to the child in the classroom. It is impossible to assess what effect a change in the environment or change of teacher, period of illness, or even the holidays may have upon the child and teachers must take time to watch, listen and talk to the child in order to try to understand how to help the child progress.

"If he can't learn the way you teach, can you teach the way he learns?" (Daphne Hamilton-Fairley: in a lecture)

It is all too easy to inherit children with a long list of things they cannot do. If the teacher is to effect change for these pupils then observational assessment is essential as a first step upon which the teacher can decide future action. This needs to focus on two main areas:

a) attitude b) skills

Changing attitude

In many cases the first help a teacher needs to provide is to persuade these children to believe that they will become readers and to show them why they need to read. Many of the children already believe that they are unable to learn and in a desperate effort to maintain some self-esteem convince themselves that they do not need to learn. The teacher must take time to change their "confirmed inadequacy" and to show them that they will succeed. This is not a quick or easy achievement but spending time observing what they can do and constantly telling the children where they are successful goes a long way to boosting their confidence. It is essential not to build upon a deficit model in which the child constantly receives the message that he/she cannot do something, but to provide reading material that the child can manage or to support the reading in such a way that the child is successful. In the past the reading material that was written for children with reading difficulties was often dull, repetitive and poorly illustrated. The children frequently endeavoured to "learn the text by heart." Today there is more chance of finding texts that the children can read and which they want to read. In order for a child to want to read he/she needs to see that others enjoy reading. Some of these children may come from homes where reading is not a highly valued activity. If these children are ever to experience the satisfaction that books can offer then it is more likely to come from an enthusiastic teacher, eager to share the pleasure of books. This does not simply mean reading an exciting story at the end of the day but reading for information, reading the environment, reading diagrams, instructions, pictures etc and highlighting the value of this "reading" to the children.

Improving basic skills

"Reading cannot be simply a guessing game. There must be some decoding of the printed text so that guesses can be confirmed or disconfirmed. Furthermore, decoding must be taught. It cannot be expected to materialise as a byproduct of intelligent guesswork." Oakhill (1988)

The starting point for effective reading is to build upon the skills already acquired. A child may be able to decode a repeated word in context but may not be able to write it unaided. In order to establish what knowledge has become automatic it is useful to check what book handling knowledge the child has, what letter names, initial letter sounds, blends or digraphs are known; how the child is forming the letters and what words the child can write from memory. This information should be carefully recorded and the child given encouragement and praise for the achievement. This should form the starting point for any future teaching building upon the knowledge the child has demonstrated.

In the 1960's the research of McNally and Murray found that approximately 100 key words accounted for about half of the total words in everyday reading material. These are words that are not necessarily phonically regular, few of them have meaning in isolation but take their meaning in the context of other words; they cannot not be represented pictorially. They are generally the vital carrier words that hold together a piece of text and which need to be recognised rapidly so that the reader can devote time to the meaning of the text which is generally provided by the nouns and verbs. If the reader has to spend time decoding these words then the chance of retaining the overall meaning of the passage is slim. Many similar lists have been suggested since the work of McNally and Murray but the first hundred words remain fairly constant. (see Section "Diagnosis and action" page 21)

Improving phonic awareness

All children need to understand letter-sound correspondence. Traditionally teachers have started work by teaching initial letter correspondence and then moved on to teaching digraphs and blends. For many young children this appeared to be an impossible task. However, there has been considerable research into how to help children to start to identify letter-sound correspondence. Bryant (1993) and Goswami (1994) have stressed the importance of rhyme for children. This larger "sound bite" is more recognisable by children and alerts them to the possibility of using analogies between spelling patterns in words when they begin to learn to read.

The child who learns how to pronounce the letter string k/ing can be shown its connection to r/ing, w/ing, br/ing. Teachers need to demonstrate to children the sound similarities between words, for example "wing and bring" and the similarities between "bring and brush" This reading by analogy, working from words and sounds that children can recognise is not the same as the traditional phonics programmes which required the child to sound out each individual letter and then try to synthesise them. Encouraging children to use analogies enables the child to work at the phonological level that is most accessible to the beginning reader. As children increase their reading ability so their ability to break the words into smaller phonological units increases. The fluent reader uses both word-letter knowledge and letter-sound knowledge to decode print into words and to help them to spell words. The research of Goswami (1994) shows that the best results are achieved when children are given phonological training in rhyming and alliteration to accompany the analogy training of grouping words with shared spelling patterns. Slow readers often appear to have poor phonological skills and research seems to suggest that they find it easier to learn to read by first recognising analogies as analogies exploit a phonological level that children find accessible.

Summary

Readers need to know:

* the words on a page contain a message and that the purpose of reading is to understand and respond to the message.

* readers have to have a clear idea **why** they are reading but they also need to be able to recognise most of the words rapidly and accurately.

* if they are unable to recognise a word they need to have clear strategies that they can use to decode that word.

Teachers need to:

handwritten note: link to literacy ladder

* read aloud to all children on a regular basis
* talk about books and discuss with children the issues raised in the stories
* demonstrate the importance they attach to reading
* observe and record what a child can do
* prepare readings and record them
* set aside time for increasing the basic sight vocabulary through the use of big books etc.
* spend time encouraging child to listen to rhyme, letter sounds and use analogies

ORGANISING RESOURCES FOR STRUGGLING READERS

Most schools say that they are seriously under-resourced with books that are suitable for children who are finding reading difficult. The range of ability and interest is likely to vary between each child. It is a daunting task to try to provide a story that will hold the interest of the reader, provide enough repetition of the words that the child can manage and at the same time offer a manageable challenge. However, it is essential that the resources that the school does possess are graded so that all the people who support the child know the progression of the different levels.

Grading Books

Trying to grade books which have a high interest level and a low reading level is an uphill task. Publishers have tried to overcome this by offering graded reading schemes but even these rarely have enough material at each level to ensure that these are all the resources that are needed to launch the struggling reader.

One suggestion has been to ask three or four colleagues to gather all the resources for grading into the staff room and to place them into four broad bands. When this has been agreed each band is looked at again and divided into two levels. This refining process can obviously continue until the teachers are satisfied that they have graded the books as finely as they wish. This also quickly identifies levels which need extra resourcing. It is tempting to think that this work can be done by one member of staff but the combined assessment of several staff has been shown to be much more accurate. If the school has chosen a "scheme" as a core of reading material for their struggling readers it is possible to match other resources to the levels of the scheme, but again this is usually more successful if more than one member of staff is involved.

Selecting resources

* When reading to the teacher or helper the struggling reader needs to complete a "whole text" in a short time. Therefore the length of the story and the number of lines on a page are important considerations.
* Struggling readers need to experience success: look at the amount of repetition within the text.
* Struggling readers often "read" the pictures to help them understand the story: look at the accuracy of the picture-word match
* Anxious children often complain of blurred text: look at the amount of spacing between the words and between the lines.
* Struggling readers will be using most of their processing capacity to decode the text: look at the clarity of the story.

Storing the resources

It is essential that all those who are working with children who are finding reading difficult know where they can find the resources and what material is linked to the resources. Schools need to discuss what and where they should store the resources. There is no easy solution and the final decision is quite likely to be dependent upon the physical lay-out of the school buildings as much as anything.

* Own Class Selection

Some schools opt for storing a limited range of resources in each classroom.

This means that the classroom teacher and any helpers in that class can easily find the resources but it is very unlikely that there are sufficient resources available for each classroom to be adequately resourced.

If the books are kept in a special place or container within the classroom it may over-emphasise the fact that some children are not reading as well as others.

* Library Shelf Collection

Some schools prefer to place the resources all together and therefore provide a wider selection but it is obvious to all the school which children need to use these resources. Also it is unlikely that follow-up resources can be displayed with the accompanying texts.

* Special Needs Room

This is quite popular as a solution and it does mean that all teachers and helpers know where to find the resources and that they are likely to have any accompanying material kept with the texts. However, other children quickly identify the room with children who are having difficulty and the struggling children themselves often feel uncomfortable either going to the room to select a resource or spending time in the room with a helper.

There is no simple solution or perfect solution to the organisation of resources for special needs. What is important is that all staff are aware of the agreed upon school policy regarding resources and that everyone works to make the chosen system as effective as possible despite its limitations.

HEARING CHILDREN READ

Hearing children read has been seen as a vital part of any reading programme in the primary years. Campbell (1988) provides a list of reasons for hearing children read:

* to help children to learn to read

* develop interest and enjoyment

* re-enforce personal relationships

* give the child practice in reading

* to develop fluency and expression

* check and develop comprehension

* diagnosis

* check on progress

* check on accuracy

* instruction

* encourage the use of contextual clues

* teaching phonics

Organisation of sessions

Some or all of these reasons are likely to be present when a teacher hears an individual child read aloud and, consequently, the use of this time is seen as of the utmost importance.

Most teachers in the junior years try to set aside 5-6 minutes to hear a child read. They perceive this as the time for "teaching" reading but there is rarely time to follow-up this reading with talk or writing. Some "scheme" resources do provide such follow-up material linked to the books and it may be possible to give this to the child to complete after hearing them read. However, the teacher often has to decide whether time should be spent on the linked writing task or whether the child should return to the activity from which they have been withdrawn.

Many teachers choose to hear reading during "Quiet Reading Time". This is because it does not remove the child from other curriculum tasks and struggling readers find it notoriously difficult to be totally engaged in reading a book of their choice for 20 - 30 minutes daily. Hearing struggling readers during this time means less interruption of the time-table and other children are also less likely to interrupt the teacher. Some teachers feel guilty about using this time as the original purpose of "Uninterrupted, Silent, Sustained Reading (USSR) was for all the class, including the teacher, to be reading quietly, but in desperation they have felt that this is the only possible opportunity to work with struggling readers on an individual basis.

Teachers know that individual time spent with a struggling reader is very precious and they are constantly seeking ways of making the most effective use of this time. If the time allocated is only 5-6 minutes a session approximately three times a week, then there is very little chance of a teacher being able to do anything more than listen to the child read. They do not have the time to assess the success of previous teaching sessions or build upon the current teaching session through discussion and linked writing work.

An alternative way of structuring time with a struggling reader might be to have only two training sessions per week but to increase the time to 10 - 15 minutes. This would enable the teacher to have a few minutes in which to introduce the book and time at the end to consolidate the specific learning through linked writing activities. This length of session provides many more teaching opportunities. It gives the teacher:

* a chance to ensure that the child has read with understanding

* more time in which to analyze the strengths and weaknesses of the reader

* time to provide activities which forge the learning links between reading and writing

* time to ensure consistency in the acquisition of new sight words

* time to select and instigate an individual phonic programme

If the teacher does not have a very clear programme of how to use time spent with an individual child it is possible for valuable minutes to be wasted as the child is uncertain about what is expected in the session and the teacher is uncertain what approach to adopt.

A priority with teachers has been to provide time that is relaxed and unthreatening but this can encourage the child to believe that there is nothing important or urgent about learning to read. Each session should be vigorous, paced and systematic. As children become used to these sessions and know what is expected of them and the form the session will take then they gain confidence and come to recognise that they will learn to read and that they have to make the necessary effort.

Ways of hearing children read

Academic research has investigated the relative success of different methods to adopt when hearing children read.

1. Miscue Analysis/ Running records

Sensitive observation of a child's oral reading has become the main way in which progress is recorded. It is now recognised that listening to children's reading errors (miscues) provides the most informative insight into the developing strategies of the readers. The original work by Goodman and Burke (1972) showed that by recording a child's delivery of the text and by categorising the "miscues" it is possible to get a picture of the child's strategies. The teacher needs to categorise the "miscues" into syntactic, semantic and grapho-phonic deviations. Once the teacher has a clearer picture of the nature of the difficulties a child is experiencing then the teacher is more able to build a remediation programme to compensate for these weaknesses. However, struggling readers frequently make errors of all kinds (semantic, syntactic and grapho-phonic) so that it is very difficult to know where to begin the remediation programme. The value of this sensitive observation lies not so much in identifying a particular area of weakness but in providing further knowledge as to what a child can and cannot do.

Advantages of Miscue Analysis

* It is a very thorough analysis of the decoding skills

* It provides insights into the cueing system a child is using

* It can be used to monitor progress

* It highlights the teaching needs of the child

* It provides a systematic and rigorous analysis of reading development

Weaknesses of Miscue Analysis

* It requires an uninterrupted time with a child

* It requires time for analysis after the miscues session

would be a problem when child has own book.

* It depends upon an appropriate match between the child and the book. Too easy a text reveals very little information but if the text is too difficult then the number or "miscues" to be analyzed is excessive and generally shows the child as weak in every aspect.

* Teachers have to learn the technique

Conclusion

* It is useful for monitoring purposes

* Its value depends on the follow- up work that is based upon the analysis

2. Paired Reading

Paired reading was first designed by Roger Morgan (1986) to meet two basic criteria. He worked with children who were finding reading difficult and he wanted to enlist the help of non-professionals and to devise a programme that was simple to administer and required the minimum of training but at the same time was flexible and could be used on a wide variety of reading material. Morgan described the approach as follows:

" Tuition is undertaken using a book of the child's choice, suitable for his or her interests and chronological age rather than being restricted to his or her reading age. Sessions begin with a parent and child reading simultaneously and aloud, the parent thus providing a continuous prompt or model for the child's reading. When a child is sufficiently confident to read a few words or a passage alone, he or she signals this by knocking on the table. The parent praises this, stops reading with the child and the child continues reading aloud alone. While the child is reading alone correctly, the parent re-enforces the correct reading by frequent praise or "feedback that you are right", using positive comments suitable for the individual child. When the child becomes stuck or makes a mistake while reading alone the parent allows approximately four seconds for further attempts. If the child is unable to resolve the problem in this time, the parent supplies the correct word, the child repeats it with the parent and simultaneous reading is resumed again until the child knocks." Morgan (1986)

Further research on Paired Reading was undertaken by Topping and Lindsay (1992) who found it to be very effective. They pointed out that the support the reader received during reading allowed the reader to deploy more processing capacity in understanding the text, it raised self- image and it enabled the struggling reader to access books well above the independent reading level of the child.

Advantages of the Paired Reading Approach

* The child is able to complete more of a book

* Some children really liked it

* It enabled the child to tackle texts that were more interesting

* It helps with fluency and intonation

Disadvantages

* Some children disliked the procedure

* It reminded them they could only read with an adult

* It disguised the cueing strategies

Conclusions

* It is suitable for some children or with some books

* It is most beneficial if the child re-reads after the paired reading.

3. The Neurological Impress Method

The Neurological Impress method was invented and designed by Gardiner (1965) who wanted to combine sight, hearing and touch together in the teaching of reading. This has similarities with the Paired Reading approach as the student and instructor read aloud together in unison. In this approach the teacher and child select a story with which the child is comfortable. The teacher introduces the story and makes a rapid judgement as to which words or phrases are likely to interfere with fluency. The child is trained to follow the print by running his or her finger under the text keeping in time with the teacher's voice. Then the teacher and child read the same text aloud together. They do this until the child is fully confident with the passage. Finally the child reads the same passage alone but with the teacher's support if necessary. The reading is usually followed by a discussion of the passage chosen.

Advantages of the Impress method

* It helps with fluency and intonation

* It allows the child to become very confident and to feel like a reader

* It speeds up the delivery of children who read painfully slowly

* It ensures that the child reads and understands the passage

* It is very supportive of the weak reader

* It is very useful for those children for whom English is a second language

Disadvantages

* Some children do not like it

* It breaks down if the text is too complex

* It requires the teacher to read at a pace that is not too fast or too slow for the child

* It does require a considerable amount of time, some children found it too intensive

Conclusions

* it works best with short texts and poetry

* It helps with delivery of texts and improves fluency

* It is useful to do occasionally to help with a specific problem

4. Pause, Prompt and Praise

This approach was developed by McNaughton, Glynn and Robinson (1980) who worked with children experiencing reading difficulty and wanted to help teachers and parents to respond to children's reading in a positive and practical way. They described the response in two ways:

* what to do when the child read correctly

* how to help when the child read incorrectly.

For correct reading the researchers were keen to encourage the parent or teacher to praise often and specifically. They suggested that children should be praised when they read a sentence correctly, when children corrected themselves after a mistake and when children got a word correct after the adult had prompted them.

When children experience problems with their reading the researchers suggested that the adult paused and waited to give the child a chance to tackle the problem without immediate interference. This pause could be as long as five seconds and many teachers have counted to ten under their breath in order to help them to hold back from prompting too early. However, if the child produces a word that does not make sense the adult should prompt with clues about the meaning of the story. This could be "You read ..... Does that make sense?" If the prompt does not elicit the correct word the adult should then provide it for the reader. If the mistake does make sense but is not the correct word the adult could prompt with clues about the look of the word, perhaps suggesting that the child look again at the letters in the word or asking about the part of the word that is wrong. If the child says nothing when he or she comes to a difficult word the adult should suggest that the child omits the word and reads on to the end of the sentence or the adult could ask the child to read the sentence again. If the word is not correct after two prompts then the adult should provide the word and encourage the child to continue reading.

This approach is neatly summarised in its title of Pause, Prompt and Praise. The emphasis is upon giving children time to solve problems independently; providing support of an appropriate kind depending on the nature of the miscue; and finally praising the child whole-heartedly for all attempts.

The value of specific praise

All those involved in supporting struggling readers are very conscious of the need to praise and encourage their efforts. However, this praise can often be of a general nature e.g. "Well done" "Good". The helper may have a clear idea of what they are praising and why but the children may be less clear about why they have received the praise. Marie Clay (1979) found that when children were praised specifically e.g."Well done, you looked carefully at the beginning of that word and worked out what the word was" or "Very Good. You tried to read ahead to help you sort out that problem word", the child had a clearer idea of what to do.

"Specific questions make your teaching more powerful" Clay (1979). Although such detailed praise may appear interruptive it gives children a clear idea of the effective strategies they are using and greater confidence to employ the same strategy again.

RESEARCH INTO THE RELATIVE MERITS OF TECHNIQUES FOR HEARING CHILDREN READ

In a small scale piece of research, which was funded by Oxford Brookes University, we sought to investigate ways in which the classroom teacher could help struggling readers. Our priority was to evaluate the most effective use of time that a teacher could spend with an individual. Frequently this time is spent hearing a child read. The purpose of our research was to explore the relative merits of different approaches when assessing a child's oral reading. We selected two schools with different socio-economic backgrounds and asked the school to identify nine children who they felt needed support. These children were not non-readers but all of them had weak reading skills. Three children were selected from Y2, three children from Y3 and three children from Y4-Y6. These children were then placed at random on one of three approaches. These approaches were: paired reading followed by a linked writing activity; prepared reading followed by a linked writing activity; self-analysis of miscues followed by a linked writing activity.

We decided to call each of these ten minute sessions a "Training Session" as they united hearing children read with a linked writing activity.

As the research was very small scale, it was not possible to claim that any one approach was better than another. What did become clear was that certain approaches suited the personality of certain children. As the research continued and the children became more confident in reading then they were more able to self-analyze their miscues and this helped them to recognise good strategies rather than "snatching" at any approach and hoping it would enable them to access the troublesome word.

Prepared Reading

In this approach the teacher and the child look through the story prior to the child attempting to read it. In this time the teacher scanned the text and noted any possible problem vocabulary. Then, when talking about the pictures and the story with the child, the teacher unobtrusively fed in the specific vocabulary. No attempt was made to alert the child to the written form of the new vocabulary but as far as possible the child was encouraged to feed back that vocabulary.

For example; the text read "The elephant went into the sports shop." The picture showed an elephant standing on skateboard surrounded by sports equipment. In preparing the vocabulary the teacher would ensure that the child said the word "elephant" when pointing to the picture and the teacher supplied the vocabulary of "sports shop" in the course of the conversation. Not too much time should be spent on this preparation as the child must also have time to complete a reading of the text and also have time for related language work. However, the priority of this approach is to share the whole story and to ensure the child has heard the new vocabulary prior to reading the text alone.

This approach allows the child to devote more of his or her "processing capacity" to decoding when reading aloud to the teacher as they already have a firm grip on the content of the story.

Advantages of Prepared Reading

* children are surprised and delighted that they can "recognise"words
* children understand the whole story
* cueing systems are evident
* children are less anxious about "problem" words
* it gives children "book language"

Disadvantages

* It can be difficult to supply the vocabulary
* Some texts do not provide enough picture clues to elicit the story

Conclusion

* it does not seem to spoil the story
* children adopted the habit of looking through a book
* it increased their sense of story
* it increased their confidence

Self-analyzing Miscues

We also explored the value of asking children to reflect upon how they managed to decode words which caused them some problem when they first came upon it in a text. In this approach, after a child had self-corrected the teacher asked the child what he or she had done in order to make the self-correction.

For example; the text was "The tiny man wanted a coat to put on". The child hesitated for some seconds before the "coat" and then correctly produced the word. The teacher asked him how he knew the word. He replied" I looked at the word and I saw the 'c' and then I looked at the next word and I knew the word was "coat". To start with the children found it quite difficult to reflect upon their actions. On many occasions they suggested that they had used techniques that were clearly improbable. This was because they were unused to analyzing their strategies. However we found that as children became more familiar with the technique they struggled to give an accurate explanation of how they had set about to decoding the word.

When the child volunteered the explanation the teacher was able to praise successful decoding techniques and discourage less successful. For example, one child told us that he always used the first three letters and tried to read the word based on the sounds these three letters made. This worked successfully on enough occasions for the child to believe it was a strategy he could always employ. We were able to discover how dependent he was upon this approach and to widen the range of decoding strategies for the child.

The advantage of this approach is that the teacher consults the child about the text when the child has successfully corrected a word. This meant that attention was drawn to something that the child was doing right rather than stressing something the child was finding difficult.

Advantages of self-analysis of miscues

* children gained confidence in cueing strategies
* teacher can praise the more productive strategies
* it provides an insight into the child's techniques

Disadvantages

* some children felt threatened by the approach
* it can seem interruptive

Conclusions

* Child begins to believe that reading is not entirely guesswork
* the approach builds upon success

The value of the tape recorder when hearing children read

Throughout the research into prepared reading and analyzing self-corrections we taped the children reading unless the child appeared anxious about the tape recorder. We placed the recorder on the table in front of the child slightly raised so that the child's voice bounced against the internal microphone. The recording was generally done in the classroom with the background noise of the other children. Although this does not achieve a very clear recording, all the recordings made could be heard and followed by the teacher and the child afterwards. In most cases the children were pleased to hear themselves and once they had got over the initial shock of hearing their own voice they would listen and follow what they had read with obvious enjoyment. Frequently they were very pleased with themselves and this boosted their confidence. They would listen to themselves and ask to read again striving to improve their fluency and phrasing. In many cases we realised that the child had no idea of the quality of their delivery and by recording and re-recording the reading the child became aware of the importance of punctuation and eventually heard themselves reading like the best of their peers.

It was important that the children did this on texts that they found interesting and which warranted multiple readings. One of the most successful resources was poetry and many of the other children in the class requested to be recorded reading poems. It was also important to establish that the child wanted to be recorded and understood why this was taking place.

The Training Session

We set aside ten minutes in which to hear a child read, to talk about the story and then to link the reading with a short writing activity.

Marie Clay (1980) found that one of the most effective ways to consolidate sight words was to encourage the child to practise writing those words that they could read within context but which were not read with complete confidence.

"When a child writes she has to know the sound-symbol relations inherent in reading. Auditory, visual and motor systems are all at work when the child writes and all contribute to a greater skill in reading" Clay (1980).

We found that if the children practised writing key words from the story they had just read then these words frequently became recognised sight words at the following training session.

After the child had read aloud to us, we selected a sentence from the book which included known written vocabulary, partially recognised sight words and some unknown words. For example, we chose the sentence, "Now I will have to fish you out." The words "I", "will", "to" and "you" were part of the child's known written vocabulary. The words we chose to consolidate were "have" and "fish". The remaining words "Now" and "out" were given to the child.

Initially, each of the words in the sentence were studied by the child. Each word was then covered in turn and the child wrote it from memory. When the whole sentence had been written the target words were worked upon. For example; in order to learn the word "have" the child first spelled aloud the word using letter names. Then the child produced the letters using his index finger on the table. Finally, the child wrote the word several times from memory on to a practice page. The word "fish" was selected in order to draw attention to the letter patterns in words. We helped the child to write the word fish and then said "You have written the word "fish" now you can write the word "dish" and "wish".

The manipulation of the initial letter sound enabled the child to begin to understand word segmentation and for many struggling readers this was the first realisation that there were patterns in words and that conquering one word enabled them to gain access to several others.

Finally the child wrote the whole sentence from memory with the exception of the two words the teacher had selected as "given" words.

An alternative use of the final 5 minutes of the training session could be to play a game which practised the relevant vocabulary or to talk about the story the child had just read. Questions that prompted response to the story need to be prepared before the training session. The work of Aidan Chambers (1993) has brought home the enormous value of sharing responses to a book. He suggests that children need to "share enthusiasms (likes and dislikes), share puzzles (i.e. difficulties with the text), share connections (i.e. connecting events or characters with events or people or characters or story from another book)" .

Typical questions could be:

"Did you guess what was going to happen in the end?"

"Which character did you like best in the story?" *make sure*

"Tell me about the bit you liked best" *they think about*

"Could this story have really happened?" *what they are*

Was there anything you did not like in this story?" *reading*

"Have you read another story like this one?"

"Has anything like the events in this story happened to you?"

The researchers found it almost impossible to think up open-ended questions on the spur of the moment and when time was pressing. It was far easier to "test" the reader by asking literal questions of recall than to pose questions which asked the reader to reflect and respond.

Questions which encourage the children to make connections between what they have read and their own lives involve children in a much broader experience of reading. It is this aspect that is so difficult to achieve with struggling readers whose own view of reading is generally so skills-dominated.

"The teacher needs to comment on what is read and evaluate the story through discussion, rather than comment on the reader and evaluate how well the text was read" Tann (1991).

Conclusion

Summary

There are a variety of supportive techniques a teacher/helper can offer struggling readers when hearing them read. Each technique has something to offer and one approach may be more valuable for one child than another. What is important is that an approach is decided upon by all those who assist the child and that it is rigorously adhered to.

The value of devising a set procedure to be undertaken in a training session is that everyone involved knows what to do (both adult and child) and what is expected of them. Very often, it is the children with the weakest reading skills who are heard to read by the greatest variety of people. Each adult involved is likely to emphasis a different focus or decoding strategy and consequently the children may become muddled and confused about exactly what to do when they come across a word they cannot read. Some helpers may give the child time to attempt to read the word, others, fearing the child may lose continuity of the story, provide the word immediately. Some helpers resort to asking the children to "sound out" the word, while others may tell them to look at the pictures.

While none of these approaches is inherently wrong, when a child receives such a variety of help it is conceivable that they are spending time trying to select the helper's preferred approach rather than gaining confidence in their own developing decoding strategies.

Providing a continuous approach to support struggling readers should be a matter for a whole school policy and made available to all helpers - parents, visitors, governors.

DIAGNOSIS AND ACTION

After hearing a child read

The value of hearing children read depends upon the quality of follow-up work undertaken as a result of discovering the nature of the child's difficulties. This follow-through from diagnosis to action is the means by which problems are identified and remedies are sought to alleviate them. Too often, time is only set aside to hear a child read without considering the consequent teaching that is needed to help the child improve. Hearing children read is **not** teaching them to read. Teachers need to have clear ideas about what to do with the insights they have gained when hearing the child read. The following suggestions are a brief list of reading opportunities that might be offered to the children between training sessions.

Diagnosis: child is not reading for meaning.

Action:

* **Sequencing:** provide the story cut up into simple sequential sentences and ask the child to read the sentences and place them in the order of the story. If the original text is very short the actual sentences from the book could be used or the teacher may need to precis the story into approximately ten sentences.

* **True or False**: The teacher writes out true or false statements about the events of the story and asks the child to read and decide to which category each sentence should belong. Providing these as separate sentences allows the child to pick them up physically and move the sentences between the two piles. This "physical" approach is usually preferred by reluctant readers and if the sentences are kept in a resources file it means they can be used on many occasions

* **Connecting "Split" Sentences:** These can either be sentences taken from the book the child is reading or ones created by the teacher. The teacher needs to write the sentences on to thin card or onto a A4 page. If these are provided already cut into strips and cut in half the child can manipulate the sections and this enables him or her to read and re-read for sense. If an A4 sheet is provided the teacher needs to divide the page down the centre and ensure that the correct sections are not adjacent to each other.

* **Joke Books**: Most simple jokes depend on either a play on words or being surprised by the final line. Reluctant readers are generally keen to tell jokes to their peers and this reading, telling and sometimes explaining consolidates the need to understand the meaning of the words.

* **Cloze Passages:** The teacher selects a passage the child can read, either from a book the child has read or the teacher writes a new passage. The teacher can select specific vocabulary deletion or delete every 12 word. The reader is asked to read the passage and replace the missing words. The child has to read with understanding and have a good grasp of syntactic knowledge to complete the passage.

* **Action Sentences**: Tell the children to work with a partner and provide them with "action" sentences. The children take it in turns to read a sentence and then follow the instruction. For example "Put your book under your chair"

* **"Read and Do" Pictures:** The teacher provides the children with a simple picture outline. For example there might be a hill, a river and a road. The teacher writes simple instructions on to the work sheet for the child to read and complete. For example "Draw a tree on the top of the hill."

* **Group Reading:** Place the struggling reader in a small group reading situation (4-6 children) and encourage the group to discuss set questions and incidents in the story.

Diagnosis: over-dependent on sounding out

Action:

* **Sight word games:** the teacher selects a limited number of sight words and writes these on to card. The words are placed face down upon the table. The child has to read and pick up the words within a given number of seconds. Alternatively the words could be written on to a pathway that runs down a base board . The child has to read the words as fast as possible. He or she may omit a word but that word is noted and offered in other reading games. N.B. The following words are generally accepted as the most common sight words.

These twelve words account for about 25% of the total words:

a and he I in is it of that the to was

The following 20 words account for about a further 10 % of the total words:

all are as at be but are for had have him his not on one said they we with you.

The following 68 words account for another 20% of the total words:

about an back been before big by call came can come could did do down first from get go has her here if into just like little look made make me more much must my no new now off old only or our other out over right see she some their them then there this two when up want well went were what where which who will your.

* **Tracking Games**: The teacher selects a page from a child's comic or magazine written in continuous prose. The teacher gives the child a highlighter pen and asks the child to mark all the times the designated sight word occurs. For example the word could be "and". The child has to learn to skim over the text but also recognise and mark the word.

* **Reading well-known tales:** select a simple well known tale and encourage the children to read it quickly. As the story is already known the reader is far more likely to take risks and "recognise" the words. This helps to break the habit of over-dependence on letter sounds.

Diagnosis: limited sight vocabulary

Action

* **"My Own Book"** : The teacher writes down dictated simple sentences provided by the child into a home-produced book. The child is encouraged to "read" the sentences to his or her friend. This has added appeal if the book has a "lift the flap" section which reveals the answer to a question. For example the child might have the repeated sentence "Have you seen my monster" written on each page and under a flap on the opposite page could be the answer "yes" or "no". The friend would have to guess whether the monster was present or not.

* **Word in the Box:** The teacher provides each member of a small group with a selected number of key sight words. The teacher then slowly reads a simple story and every time any sight word is mentioned the child holding that word has to say"Stop" and place their word in the box.

* **Dominoes:** The teacher makes a set of dominoes with two high usage sight words written on each card. Each word needs to be repeated four times but it can be linked with other sight words or have two identical words on the card. Two children play by dividing the cards and then playing like dominoes where they match the word on the card that is on the table with one in their hand, but they have to read the word correctly before being allowed to place the card down on the table.

* **Turn and read:** The teacher makes a set of cards containing the sight words she wants the children to practise. The cards are laid face down on the table. The children take it in turns to select a card and read it. If they are correct they may keep the word. If they are incorrect the card is returned to the table and placed face down. The winner is the child with the most cards at the end. Care must be taken that the players can recognise a good proportion of the sight words and are only presented with a few troublesome words.

* How many can you get? The teacher selects three different coloured sheets of paper and cuts them up into 1" x 2" strips. She writes the sight words appropriate to the players onto the cards. The words are placed into three different boxes according to their colour. The players take it in turns to select a box and take out all the cards. The player then endeavours to read as many words as possible. When the player reads a word incorrectly the play is stopped and all words that remain unread, plus the incorrect word, are returned to the box. The player may keep those words correctly read. The next player selects a box and tries to read as many as possible of the words. Play continues until all the words have been read. The winner is the player with the most words. N.B. There needs to be several cards with the same word written on them to ensure that the players meet the words several times.

Diagnosis: poor word segmentation

Action:

* Spelling games: The teacher gives the child a simple letter string and then asks the child to try to make as many words using that string as possible. For example The string could be "ing" The child should try to make words "k/ing w/ing str/ing". The child should be encouraged to sound the initial letter sound and the letter string as he or she writes them.

* Push the counter: Tell the child to listen to a selected polysyllabic word and to split that word into the different segments. The child should push a counter up the table for each syllable. For example; the word could be "teddy" . The child breaks this into two syllables and pushes a counter for the initial syllable "ted" and a second counter for "dy"

* Clap the syllable: The teacher says a polysyllabic word slowly and carefully. The children listen to the word and then clap the corresponding number of syllables. A good starting point can be the child's own name. Finally the child should say the word stressing the split into the different syllables.

Diagnosis: won't guess at unknown words

Action:

* Paired reading: Encourage the child to read with another adult or peer and explain that they are to read simultaneously.

* Read Along Audio tapes: Provide the child with a recording of a suitable text and ask the child to read along with the recording. Encourage the child to run his or her finger under the words as they are read. These tapes may be made by older children in the school, a willing parent or teacher or be professionally made.

* **Prepared Reading:** The teacher or helper could prepare the vocabulary of the story by using the prepared approach.

Diagnosis: guesses wildly or omits words

Action:

* **Shared reading:** The teacher shares the reading of a text with a small group of children drawing attention to the need for accuracy. Using a "Big Book" text can ensure that all the group both see and partake in the shared read.

* **Sight Vocabulary Games**: The teacher needs to select words that are causing some problem to the reader and encourage the child to practise these words by playing the games as described on page 23.

* **Easier texts:** The child may have selected a text that is too difficult and start guessing wildly, often by "reading the pictures". Suggest that the child selects another book or ask the child to record simple texts for younger readers on to tape. In this case, the reader must read carefully and accurately.

* **Neurological Impress method:** The teacher selects an appropriate text for concentrated re-readings. (For a fuller description of this approach see page 12)

* **Skipping Words:** If the child constantly omits words he or she should be encouraged to point to the words as he reads the text. This approach should only be allowed to continue for a very limited time as this can cause the reader to read in a monotonous and stilted way. However the reader does need to recognise the importance of reading all the words.

* **Recording reading:** Record the child reading to you and then provide the child with a copy of the passage. The child should listen to the recording and circle the words omitted. Encourage the child to reread the passage onto the tape a second time, allowing the child to attempt to read all the words.

Diagnosis: ignores punctuation

Action:

* **Punctuation in Big Books:** Use a "Big Book" version with a group of children and draw attention to the punctuation. Encourage the group to join in with the text when the punctuation indicates that the characters are speaking.

* Audio tapes/ read along: Encourage the child to listen to a well-read text and to notice the use the reader makes of punctuation. Let the child try to read a small section of the text on to tape and practice reading with intonation and attention to the punctuation

* Group reading: provide four children with copies of Plays suitable for small groups. Encourage them to read with expression and intonation. Point out the place and importance of punctuation when reading aloud.

* Group Writing: The teacher or helper should act as a scribe to a small group who are responsible for creating a "group story" The teacher needs to explain the punctuation he or she is using in the group writing or ask the group what punctuation is needed for their story.

Diagnosis: inadequate phonic knowledge

Action:

* Check known phonic knowledge: In order to check the phonic knowledge the teacher should examine the spelling errors that the child has made in "free" writing. Further information can be gained by asking the child to write words starting with sounds that may not have occurred within the writing. Finally the teacher should check how far the child is able to link an initial letter or blend with a simple short vowel. For example, "ba be bi bo bu".

* Think of a word: The teacher needs to provide a card for each letter of the alphabet. The cards are laid face down in rows on the table. The players take it in turns to pick up a card. They then have to think of a word that starts with the letter or blends written on the card. If they do this they keep the card. If they cannot think of a word the card is handed to the player on the left who is given approximately five seconds to think of a word. The card continues from player to player until a correct word has been given. The winner is the player with the most cards.

* Word trail: The teacher or helper asks the first child to suggest a word and the teacher writes the word down. The next player has to think of a word that starts with the sound of the last letter of the previous player. Play continues with the adult writing the words and the players using the last letter written as the starting sound for the next word.

* Rhyming: The teacher either reads rhyming verses to the group and asks them to identify the rhyming words or provides simple rhyming couplets for the group or individual to complete. For example, "We went far, in Dad's ..."
"We saw a frog, sitting on a ..."
"Obey the rules on a farm, and you will come to no ...."

Diagnosis: does not attempt to read silently

Action:

* Using the cartoon strip

Select a short cartoon story which has blocks of simple text provided under the pictures. Explain to the children that you want them to browse through the story and read it silently

Ask the children to tell you the story but do not let them read aloud the text.

Talk about how and why people read silently.

* Sequencing

Provide two copies of a cartoon script. Cut one into separate pictures and if possible mount on to card and laminate. Ask the child to read the whole story silently and then ask the child to sequence the cut up pictures without reference to the complete sheet.

* What's missing?

Ask the child to read the story using the complete sheet. Place the separate cards down on the table in sequential order. Remove two or three cards and hand them to the child. Ask him or her to put them back in the correct place. An alternative is to remove the cards and ask the child to identify the missing cards and tell you what was on them.

N.B. Children who insist on reading aloud need to realise that they can understand the text without having to "hear" it. These activities are designed to build up their confidence after they have read silently. Comic strips such as Rupert Bear are a useful resource for these activities.

References

Arnold H. (1982) Listening to Children Read. Hodder and Stoughton

Bentley D. & Reid D. (1994) Unpublished research funded by Brookes University

Bryant P. (1993) "Phonological aspects of Learning to Read". In Beard R. Teaching Literacy: Balancing the Perspectives. Hodder and Stoughton

Campbell R. (1988) Hearing Children Read. Routledge

Chambers A. (1993) Tell Me. The Thimble Press

Clay M. (1975) What did I Write? Heinemann Educational Books

Clay M (1979) The Early Detection of Reading Difficulties. Heinemann

Clay M. (1980) "Early Writing and Reading: Reciprocal Gains". In M Clark & T Glynn (ed) Reading and Writing for the Child with Difficulties. Occasional Publications Number Eight. University of Birmingham

Gardiner C. (1965) Experimental use of the Impress Method of Reading Habilitation.

Co-operative Reading Project. US Office of Education 003838

Goodman Y. & Burke C. (1972) Reading Miscue Inventory. Macmillan

Goswami U. (1994) "The Role of Analogies in Reading Development". In Support for Learning Vol 9 No.1

McNally J. & Murray W. (1965) Key Words for Literacy and the Teaching of Reading. Schoolmaster Publishing Company

McNaughton S., Glynn T., & Robinson V. R. (1980) Parents as Remedial Reading Tutors. Issues for Home and School. New Zealand Council for Educational Research

Medwell J. (1991) "What do children think about reading - does it matter?" In Harrison C. & Ashworth A. (eds) Celebrating Literacy, Defending Literacy. Blackwell

Meek M. (1991) On Being Literate. Bodley Head

Morgan R. (1986) Helping Children Read. Methuen

Oakhill J. (1988) Becoming a Skilled Reader. Blackwell

Stanovitch K. (1980) "Toward an Interactive, compensatory model of individual differences in the Development of Reading Fluency". Reading Research Quarterly 16 32-71

Tann S (1991) Developing Language in the Primary Classroom. Cassell

Topping K., & Lindsay G. A. (1992) The Structure and development of the Paired Reading   Technique". In Journal of Research in Reading 15 (2) 120 - 136